SUPER SCIENTISTS

# THE
# BRIGHT IDEA

## ANN MOORE

*Illustrated by Mike Adams*

MACDONALD YOUNG BOOKS

# The sound of magic

Marion tapped on the transmitter over and over again. Dot dash dash dot – dot dash. Dot dash dash dot – dot dash. The Morse Code spelt the letters PA. Marion sighed impatiently as she waited for her pa. He said he had a surprise and she wanted to see it.

"Oh Dot, do be quiet!" He suddenly appeared in the doorway.

Marion's father was the famous American scientist, Thomas Edison. Because he'd worked with Morse Code transmitters for many years, he'd nicknamed her Dot. Her brother Tom was Dash.

"Hurry up!" Marion tugged Edison's hand. "I want to see the surprise in the laboratory."

Marion ran along beside Pa as they crossed the grass to the long wooden laboratory. They hurried upstairs to join Edison's assistants round a workbench. Marion smiled excitedly at everyone.

"There!" Edison swept a cover off the end of the bench. Marion felt disappointed. Was this the surprise? All she could see was a solid metal tube wrapped in tinfoil, with a handle through it. A needle from a smaller tube at the side had made marks on the tinfoil.

"Ready?" Pa turned the handle.

*Mary had a little lamb, its fleece was white
as snow.*

Marion heard Pa's voice. Then she
watched him sneeze, but the rhyme didn't
stop. How could Pa sneeze and yet go on
speaking at the same time? He turned
the handle faster and his
voice went higher.
It must be a
trick!

Pa's engineer, Charles Batchelor, laughed at Marion's puzzled expression.

"It's a phonograph!" he announced. "Your father has invented an amazing machine which records sounds and then plays them back."

"What we say today, we could listen to again and again, Dot!"

Pa couldn't hide his excitement. "Think how useful that could be," he said as he patted the machine. "This baby's going to be very important!"

"Can I have a go?" asked Marion shyly.

For an hour Marion and her father played with the phonograph. She recorded a poem and everyone cheered when it was played back.

Then Edison frowned and scratched his head. "Electricity," he said thoughtfully. "I wonder if our phonograph could be worked by electricity?" He turned back to the bench, and Marion knew he'd forgotten all about her.

# All about Pa

Late one night, Marion crept into the laboratory alone. A single gas lamp burned near the bench where her father sat, staring at a glass globe. Dodging past benches cluttered with instruments and books, she hurried over to him. "Pa!"

Startled, Edison dropped his pencil. It rolled into the shadows. "Dot! What are you doing here? You should be in bed." He looked cross.

"Sorry, Pa," Marion said quietly, "I know you're busy, but I've got something to show you. Look!" Marion pushed her school report into his hands. She watched closely as her father read the report.

"Well done!" he said at last. "You've done much better than I ever did at school."

"But you're really clever!" cried Marion in amazement.

"Hmmm," sighed Pa. "I'm afraid my teachers didn't think so – they said I was too stupid, so your gran taught me at home. She even let me have a laboratory in our cellar. And that's when I started to invent things…"

"Did an experiment make you deaf?" Marion asked. She knew he didn't hear well.

15

"No. I sold newspapers on the railroad when I was younger. Once, I nearly missed a train and someone pulled me aboard by my ears. I'm sure that made me deaf! That's why I improved Bell's telephone – so that I can hear it better. Now, isn't it time that you were in bed?"

"What's this?" Marion picked up the globe, pretending not to hear him.

"Careful!" Edison breathed a sigh of relief when it was safely in his hands. "It's my glow bulb, something I've been working on for years. And so has Joseph Swan in England. We want to light rooms using electricity instead of gas."

"How?" asked Marion. Sometimes her father had the strangest ideas.

"Well," he explained, "first we take all the air out of a bulb like this to make a vacuum. Then a current of electricity passes through a filament inside…"

17

"What's a filament?"

"It's a thin length of metal or carbon. The electricity makes the filament so hot that it lights up. Trouble is, I don't know what to use to make a strong enough filament."

Marion thought for a minute. "String? That doesn't break."

Edison laughed. "No, that wouldn't work. It has to be very thin and able to stand very high temperatures." They both stared at the globe in silence, before Edison looked pointedly at the clock.

"All right, I'm going," said Marion reluctantly and went to bed.

# There must be a way

While Marion slept, her father returned to his problem.

"The filament," he muttered. He tugged his right eyebrow, something he often did when he was thinking. "I've tried burning strips of paper, wood, corn stalks to make carbon filaments, but none of them work. There must be a way – there must be something we haven't thought of." He tugged his eyebrow again.

He was still there at eight o'clock the next morning when Charles Batchelor arrived. Charles, a British engineer, was Edison's right-hand man at the laboratory. "Good morning!" he said, then stopped and stared.

On the bench a large light bulb was glowing faintly.

"I've done it!" shouted Edison. "An electric light bulb with a filament of thin platinum! The light isn't steady, but it lasts longer than anything else we've tried. We'll have to make it stronger, of course."

"Congratulations!" Batchelor grinned and shook his hand vigorously.

"And we must improve the globe too."
Edison paced the floor. "The size will affect
the light, and the vacuum must be as good
as possible. Any air inside and the filament
burns out too quickly."

"But what about Joseph Swan?" Batchelor
interrupted. Joseph Swan, the British
physicist, had been trying to make an
electric light bulb for years.

Edison stopped pacing. "As far as I know," he said, "he hasn't made a successful light bulb – yet."

"Then you must apply for a patent right away!" exclaimed Batchelor. "Then no one else can steal your idea."

A few months later, Batchelor burst into the laboratory waving a newspaper. "Look," he said. "It says that Swan has demonstrated a light bulb in England. His filament was made of silk thread, but it only glowed for a few minutes. Do you think we'll be the first to make the perfect light bulb now?"

# The race is on

"Pa, are you coming on the picnic?" It was the Sunday after 4 July and Marion was hoping that he'd spend the day with them again. They'd had a terrific time on Independence Day with firecrackers and paper hats. After dinner Pa had played the organ and everyone had sung.

Now, however, Pa shook his head.

"Sorry, Dot, not today – I've got far too much work to do. I must solve some problems with the glow bulb. It will only burn for a few minutes, but I want to be the first to make it burn for hours, even months," he said thoughtfully. "I know all the ways that don't work, but not the one that does!" And with that, he wandered out of the room.

All summer, Pa worked on his electric light bulb. He and his assistants tried to improve the bulb's shape and vacuum. They tried to find the best shape for the filament. And they tried to make it stronger.

"We've also got to find a way of dividing the electric current between the lamps," Edison told his assistants. "At the moment, if one goes out, they all go out. That's no use! If we're going to invent something, it's got to be useful to everyone and something everyone can afford."

One evening, Marion and her mother took Pa his supper. They found him asleep with his head on the workbench. "We won't wake him," Ma whispered as they left quietly. "He'll just go on working when he wakes. That's the way he is." And she smiled.

# Little globes of sunshine

One October morning, a year after he had patented his light bulb, Edison burst into the kitchen. "I want a large bobbin of cotton," he demanded.

"What's it for?" Marion asked as he took the bobbin.

"Just an experiment," her father answered. He turned abruptly and was gone.

Marion felt cross. Why was she never allowed to help?

Across in the laboratory, Edison said to
Batchelor, "Right. Platinum won't do. It's
not bright enough. Swan used silk thread,
we'll try cotton."

For two days and nights Edison and
Batchelor tried to make a filament by baking
lengths of cotton into carbon threads. Time
and time again the threads broke, but still
they went on trying. On the morning of
the third day, Batchelor whispered at
last, "I've done it. Let's put it in
the globe." Very carefully,
he and Edison
carried the
filament to the
globe – and
it broke.

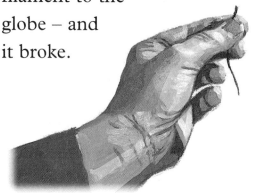

"Oh dear," Edison groaned. "Thinking of an idea is easy. It's making it work that's hard!"

After many more hours they had made another filament, but it broke again. Evening came, but they worked on.

After tea on that third day Marion decided
that she must see what Pa was doing. She
crept silently into the laboratory. Pa and
Batchelor bent over their glow bulb. Marion
tiptoed nearer and hid beneath a bench.

Her father carefully balanced a fine thread in the globe. Batchelor pumped out all the air and sealed the bulb.

"Third time lucky," she heard Pa say. "Switch it on."

A pale light glowed. "More current." The current was increased and still the bulb burned steadily. Marion jumped out of her hiding place.

"Hooray!" she shouted, and her father was so pleased with his experiment that he forgot to be cross with her for sneaking in. The bulb glowed for hours before it burned out. And the next bulb burned for even longer!

"If it can burn for forty hours, I can make it last a hundred!" Edison exclaimed.

"Ma, look how many people there are!" Marion stood at the window. A steady stream of visitors walked past on their way to the laboratory. So many people had asked to see Edison's new light bulb, that he'd opened his workshop to the public.

Inside, Edison spoke to newspaper
reporters, while machines made light bulbs
faster than any human could.

"Gee," said one reporter. "These bulbs are
like little globes of sunshine."

"Yes sir," agreed an old man nearby. He
peered at the bulb. "But I can't work out
how you get that red-hot wire in there."

Edison and Batchelor, remembering what
a struggle they'd had, smiled at each other.

# The 'universal lamplighter'

For a while, Edison continued to work on his electric light. But as usual, he was busy with other ideas as well.

"Wheee!" Marion and Tom clung together as Pa's latest invention bumped along a newly laid track beside the workshops. They were squashed beside Pa, as he drove a small electric train round the grounds.

"Hold on tight," he shouted. "We're travelling at 25 miles an hour – and I can make it go faster!" Behind him, a group of laboratory workers and newspaper reporters jolted about in an open wooden carriage. Then the train stopped. "Nearly three-quarters of a mile!" Pa beamed at everyone. "Electricity! There are so many ways it will help us if we use it properly."

Two years later Edison's electric lights had been exhibited in France and England, and even used on a ship.

"Today is the greatest adventure of my life," he said to Marion. "Today, 4 September 1882, I open the first commercial electric power station in America. It will light bulbs in more than two hundred buildings here in Pearl Street, New York."

At three o'clock that afternoon the generators hummed. Would they make enough electricity? Everyone held their breath. Then bulbs glowed and everyone cheered. The electric light age had really begun.

Soon, electric power was being supplied to homes, hotels, theatres and mills.

"Look Pa, you're famous."

Proudly, Marion held out the New York Times. "They're calling you the universal lamplighter!"

# *Epilogue*

Edison died in 1931. After his funeral,
Marion watched as all the lights of America
dimmed for a minute in memory of her
father. Even the Statue of Liberty's torch
went out. Then electricity hummed again
and lights blazed everywhere. America and
the world knew just how much they owed to
Thomas Edison and his study of electricity.

# Timeline

Thomas Edison was born on 11 February 1847 in Milan, Ohio, USA

| | |
|---|---|
| **1855** | Edison leaves school after three months. |
| **1863** | Becomes an apprentice telegrapher, work he continues until 1868. |
| **1871** | Develops Scholes' typewriter. Marries Mary Stilwell. |
| **1872** | Daughter Marion is born. |
| **1876** | Builds his laboratory at Menlo Park, New Jersey. Son Thomas is born. |
| **1877** | Improves the telephone. Tests the phonograph. |
| **1879** | Patents the light bulb. |
| **1880** | Joseph Swan patents his light bulb. Edison carries out the electric railway experiment at Menlo Park. |

| 1882 | Pearl Street Generating Station is switched on. |
|---|---|
| 1891 | Patents the kinetoscope. |
| 1899 | Begins work on electric car batteries. |
| 1912 | Works with Henry Ford to invent a self-starter for Ford's cars. |
| 1914-1918 | Works with the US Navy to develop torpedo detection. |
| 1927 | Sets up a laboratory in Florida to research rubber. |
| 1928 | Awarded a Gold Medal by Congress for his work and inventions. |

Thomas Edison died on 18 October 1931 in New Jersey, USA. He was 84 years old.

# Glossary

current — a flow of electricity

electricity — a form of energy which uses tiny particles called electrons

filament — a thin metal wire, or coil of wire, which glows red or even white-hot when electric current flows through it

generator — a machine used for changing movement into electricity

kinetoscope — the first machine to show moving pictures. It moved images on strips of film so fast that figures on them seemed to move.

laboratory — a building or room used for scientific experiments and research

patent — a document giving someone the sole right to make or sell an invention

phonograph — a machine for recording and playing back sounds. Edison first used a tube, but later sound was recorded on flat discs.

transmitter — a piece of equipment or a machine which sends out signals or messages

vacuum — a space from which all or most of the air has been removed

If you have enjoyed this storybook, why not try these other titles in the Super Scientists series:

### The Mysterious Element by Pam Robson

*Marie Curie* was a very unusual scientist – a woman! Determined to prove that she is as good as a man, she earns two university degrees, before embarking on her most exciting adventure – the search for radium.

### Heavens Above by Kenneth Ireland

*Galileo Galilei* has had a brilliant idea for a telescope – the only problem is, someone else thought of it first! And as for his ideas about the Earth travelling around the Sun…The Pope is not amused.

### The Cosmic Professor by Andrew Donkin

Eddie can't believe that he's met *Albert Einstein*, the most famous professor in the world. And he's amazed when Einstein offers to explain the secrets of the universe. Is Outer Space all it seems?

### The Explosive Discovery by Roy Apps

When *Alfred Nobel* moves to San Remo, the villagers are curious. Who is he? Where is he from? And what causes the explosions in his laboratory? His maid Maria is determined to find out…

### The Colour of Light by Meredith Hooper

What is light and what colour is it? *Isaac Newton* isn't sure, but he wants to find out. So he buys a prism, holds it up to a beam of light and a wonderful rainbow shimmers before his eyes… What *can* this mean?

Storybooks are available from your local bookshop or can be ordered direct from the publishers. For more information about Storybooks, write to: *The Sales Department, Macdonald Young Books, 61 Western Road, Hove, East Sussex, BN3 1JD.*